SCARLET ROBIN
Pentax, 400mm, 1/25th sec, f5.6, Ektachrome

Peter

Dedicated to Pat
who as wife and mother
inspired the pictures in this book

PETER SLATER · RAOUL SLATER

PHOTOGRAPHING AUSTRALIA'S

BIRDS

MORNING LIGHT, FEMALE RED-BACKED FAIRY-WREN, MOGGILL STATE FOREST, QUEENSLAND
Hasselblad ELM, 250mm, 1/500th sec, f5.6, two front flashes, one backlight, one background flash

Raoul

FOREWORD

It seems fitting that I should have met Peter Slater in a photographic processing shop.

There were two photographs on the wall. I was admiring one, a picture of a wren, when I noticed the person admiring the other, which happened to be one of mine. We got into conversation and I found out that the wren picture was his. So we became friends through mutual appreciation and have remained friends in the 20 years since. Probably, each of us is still the other's greatest fan and in subsequent years the walls of my home have become decorated with his paintings and drawings.

I also came to know Raoul well as he was growing up – even in his early teens he had an understanding of my sort of photography that I have rarely encountered elsewhere. We had many discussions about our art, and I was not surprised when he began winning international awards for his pictures at a very early age, nor to hear that he was writing a regular column on nature photography for the Australian Photographic Society while still at school.

I am delighted to have this opportunity of introducing such a fine selection of masterly pictures illustrating the art of bird photography. The Slaters seem to think that it is all quite simple, but from experience I know it is not. What is required is an incredible degree of dedication, but I agree with them that, despite the often tedious hours of patient pursuit, it is among the most enjoyable of occupations.

I commend this book to you and hope, as they do, that you may feel inspired to try your hand at photographing birds.

Steve Parish

YELLOW ROBIN COURTSHIP FEEDING, MOGGILL STATE FOREST, QUEENSLAND
Hasselblad ELM, 250mm, 25mm extension tube, 1/125th sec, f5.6, Ektachrome 64, two front flashes, one backlight, one on background

Raoul

INTRODUCTION

Photographing a bird is easy: find one, point the camera and press the shutter. Doing it well is much more difficult. The essentials are to take the picture in flattering light and to use a tripod to steady the camera, move close, move closer and then move closer still.

Taking an outstanding image becomes so difficult that the effort is painfully pleasurable and the rare reward intensely satisfying. Choose a bird in fine plumage, consider its pose and background, balance all elements into a pleasing composition and select the exposure which best expresses your vision. Then take one step closer. However, to be truly successful, the photographer also needs sympathy and love for the subject. This book is about taking those physical and emotional steps closer.

Why do we choose to photograph birds, subjects that are notoriously fickle and furtive? The answer is clear to me each time I catch my breath as a bird comes into focus on the ground-glass screen. Birds are beautiful and wild creatures. In photographing them, two instincts are being satisfied - the civilised appreciation of beauty and the primitive desire for the chase. To photograph is to hunt. The techniques for approaching the prey are similar and there is a shared vocabulary – for example, capture, aim, fire and shoot. There is the exhilaration of the chase but, at its end, instead of a head on the wall there is a framed print.

A certain satisfaction comes from holding a jewel-like transparency up to the light. However, there is much more than the end result to give enjoyment to the bird photographer. The exercise and the outdoors themselves are exhilarating. There is also mental challenge in capturing the image while making sure the welfare of the subject is always kept in mind.

Most important, we have found that the pursuit of photos brings wonderful companionship, with each other and with family and friends. Bird photography would appear to be a reclusive pastime, but in fact lends itself to partnership. Sharing the whole experience makes the final photographs simply the icing on a delicious cake.

When we set out to photograph a bird, we use simple techniques that are the culmination of years of practice based on trial and error in the field and ruthless criticism of the results. We don't have any secret or complicated methods. In these few pages, we will discuss the most productive of these techniques, indicating how we use natural light, artificial light, the mixture of these known as synchro-sun, hides, towers and stalking.

We hope that you like these photos and stories. Even more, we hope that you will be inspired to try photographing birds. Go gently, step closer and don't be discouraged if the bird flies away. Birds do that. Enjoy watching your subject fly out of reach, then try again.

Raoul

11

MASKED PLOVER, RUM JUNGLE, NORTHERN TERRITORY
Canon F1, 500mm, 1/125th sec, f4.5, Ektachrome Elite 100

Raoul

NATURAL LIGHT

This plover was photographed as the early morning sun broke through a blanket of clouds. The light up to that time had been flat and grey, making for a colourless scene and requiring a shutter speed of 1/30th second. Normally, I wouldn't bother photographing in such conditions, but the perfect reflections gave me hope for something special. I took two rolls of photos, all unsharp, victims of camera shake (the best of these pictures is reproduced on page 160). A rift then appeared in the clouds. The scene took on a beautiful glow and the shutter speed jumped to 1/125th second. I smiled to myself, snapped this photo to warm up and prepared to have some fun in the improved conditions. To my dismay, the plovers suddenly tired of their bathing and trotted off out of sight.

Most of the photos that we like, our own and other people's, were taken with long telephoto lenses by available light during the "magic hours" at sunrise and sunset. Light at these times is soft and full of warmth. Also, birds tend to be more active early and late in the day. Closer to midday, the sun casts hard shadows and scenes have too much contrast to be photogenic. Overcast days are exceptions, because the cloud cover acts as one huge light source and reflects into the shadowed areas. Photos taken during overcast conditions are soft and neutral in tone.

The best light also happens to be the dimmest. To maintain a correct exposure as light levels drop, either the aperture must be opened up or the shutter speed made slower. We prefer to use the fastest possible shutter speed, because this stops any movement made by the bird. This fast shutter speed necessitates the use of the widest aperture possible. Using an open aperture also makes the background go out of focus, a pleasing effect that separates the bird from any distracting objects behind it. These two desirable effects, maximum shutter speed and blurring of the background, have prompted us to almost make a rule for natural light photography: use a wide-open aperture. (With a lot of modern cameras, this is easily done by using a "sports" function, or switching to aperture priority and dialling in the aperture with the lowest number.) Of course, rules are made to be broken, and an example of this can be seen on the following two pages, where a closed aperture was used to slow the shutter speed, achieving a feeling of movement.

We find that in the sort of light that we like, the fastest shutter speed possible is somewhere between 1/2 second to 1/125th second. With a lens over 100mm in focal length, camera movement during these exposures will be discernible as a blurring of detail. The only solution is to use a support - a tripod, beanbag, tree branch or window sill. Here lies "almost rule" number two: use a tripod. Sometimes a tripod is too cumbersome in the bush and a handheld photo will come out sharp. Witness Dad's robin photo on the back cover of this book, taken while lying prone under a bush, but realise that such "luck" is rare.

An old camera club rule, and a good one to break, is to have the sun shining over your shoulder and onto the subject. This light is the strongest, but also the flattest. Having the sun to the side of, or behind, the subject emphasises its outline and texture in the most pleasing way. A majority of the photos in this book break the camera club rule and have at least some of the light shining towards the camera. We prefer backlighting and can invariably be found walking into the sunset looking for birds.

Raoul

SANDPIPERS, BROOMSHEAD, NEW SOUTH WALES
Canon AE1, 100-300mm zoom, 1/15th sec, f22, Kodachrome 64

14

Raoul

TAWNY FROGMOUTH AND CHICKS, KANGAROO GULLY, QUEENSLAND
Mamiya RB67, 250mm, 1/500th sec, f11, Fujichrome 100, two front flashes

FLASHLIGHT PHOTOGRAPHY

Frogmouths are nocturnal birds and become active only after dark. The bird shown here nested in the same spot for a number of years and became quite used to us. Raoul spent many nights taking pictures of it and its mate, using two electronic flashes to provide lighting. He set up the flashes, one on each side of the camera about two metres from the nest, settled into the hide in the evening and focused while it was still light. After dark, a torch covered by a red filter was used to see what was going on, based on the theory that night birds have little or no vision at the red end of the spectrum. It seemed to work.

The Forest Kingfisher overleaf was one of five birds attending their nest in a termitarium and was lit entirely by flash. Two flash heads were pointed at the nest, another was above and behind the bird as a spotlight, and two more heads were aimed at the leaves in the background. The flashes fired at about 1/5000th of a second, freezing the kingfisher's movement.

About half of the pictures in this book were taken with the aid of electronic flashes. We employ two ways of using them - firstly when the entire picture including the background is lit by artificial light, and secondly when the flash light and natural light are balanced, a technique called "synchro-sun" which we discuss on page 21.

The art of using flashes is to strive for a result that looks like natural light. We have found that it can only be done consistently by using more than one flash head. If only one is used a harsh shadow, which looks ugly and unnatural, is thrown by the bird, so a minimum of two is used, each placed so that it eliminates the shadow thrown by the other.

More often we use other flash heads both as spotlights and to light up the background - those extra heads are independent of the camera and may be as much as 30 metres away. Each is attached to a photocell which activates instantaneously when the flashes connected to the camera are fired. Once they are all set up, we take a polaroid shot to check the lighting and adjust the flashes if necessary.

Apart from being a portable sun, enabling pictures to be taken in any lighting conditions, the main virtue of electronic flash is the speed it is capable of, freezing any action, including rapidly beating wings. Our equipment is capable of speeds between 1/3000th and 1/40 000th of a second. Without such power, it would be impossible to photograph small birds in flight, such as the warbler on page 132 and the pardalotes on pages 133 and 134.

Until recently, flashes were suitable only for close work up to about four metres. Innovations such as the fresnel screen incorporated in modern flashes throw a beam considerable distances, making possible shots like the Barking Owl on page 90, taken from about 15 metres.

Peter

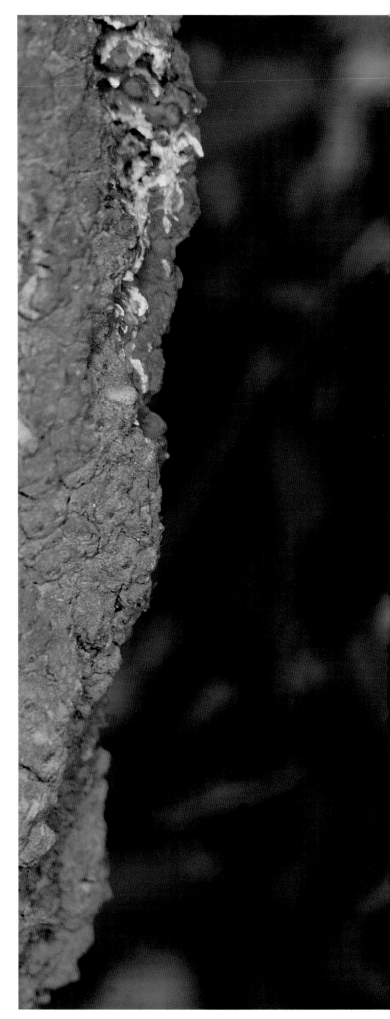

Frozen in space/time

waiting for the book to close

to finish its flight

Peter

FOREST KINGFISHER, MOGGILL, QUEENSLAND (*Peter*)
Mamiya RB67, 250mm, 1/250th sec, f5.6, Ektachrome,
two front flashes, one backlight, two flashes on background

SPOTTED HARRIERS, ASHBURTON RIVER, WESTERN AUSTRALIA
Praktisix, 180mm, 1/25th sec, f11, Ektachrome, Multiblitz two heads

Peter

SYNCHRO-SUN

This Spotted Harrier's nest was situated in a eucalypt overhanging the banks of the Ashburton River. For most of the day the nest was in shade and the opposite bank of the river was in full sunlight. To get a balanced picture, I took a light meter reading on the sunlit bank and then calculated the distance the flash heads should be placed from the nest to provide the same amount of light, in this case two metres. Then it was a matter of sitting in the hide waiting for the harriers to return, and hoping the calculations were correct.

This method of photography is called "synchro-sun", because the flashlight is synchronised with the sun. In most cases it gives better results than using flash on its own. Modern flash units can be set to provide exactly the amount of light required, so are much more efficient than the antiquated and bulky system I used for the harriers. An example of synchro-sun using modern equipment is the Pheasant Coucal overleaf. Some modern cameras have an inbuilt synchro-sun capability, automatically balancing flash and sunlight.

Problems arise when the background is not lit by sunlight, and is relatively dark. There are two possible scenarios: firstly when the nest is lit by sunlight - in this case, we use the flash on the background, and secondly, when the nest is in shadow and the background is too far away to be lit - we then adjust the flashes to provide just a touch of light on the nest, and usually put a spotlight in to highlight the bird (an example is the Willy Wagtail on page 154). The virtue of using flash in these low-light situations is that it freezes any action that takes place, even when a slow shutter speed is used.

Peter

PHEASANT COUCAL, ANSTEAD, QUEENSLAND
Mamiya RB 67, 360mm, 1/125th sec, f8, Ektachrome, two front flashes

HIDES

RED-NECKED AVOCET FLICKING WATER, CUNNAMULLA, QUEENSLAND   *Raoul*
Canon F1, 500mm, 1/250th sec, f8, Kodachrome 64

HIDE SET UP AT AVOCET NEST, CUNNAMULLA, QUEENSLAND   *Raoul*
Note hide tied to stop it flapping

The biggest hurdle to overcome in photographing birds is getting close enough. A very productive method is to employ a "hide" near a place frequented by birds, such as a nest, waterhole, food source or roost. A hide is any structure that keeps the photographer hidden from his quarry. In the picture above is a hide made from a wool-bale from which Raoul photographed the two birds pictured on these pages. The avocet shown is returning to its nest on a small island in a lake (see also page 49). It is performing a particular display, flicking water up with its bill, the purpose of which is to fool any watching predators that it is feeding and not returning to a vulnerable nest. The plover opposite visited the island frequently and was probably claiming it as territory.

The hide was introduced first about 50 metres from the island, so the avocets could get used to its alien shape. It was securely tied down so there was no chance of it flapping in the wind. After a few days it was moved a bit closer and after about five days was in position three metres from the nest. When Raoul went to photograph, I accompanied him to hasten the setting-up process and walked conspicuously away so the birds assumed all was clear. When he had the shots he wanted, he carefully poked a handkerchief out of the back. I was about half a kilometre away and returned to help Raoul emerge from the hide. This courtesy prevents the parent bird from being shocked by the sudden emergence of the photographer a few metres away. While we were preparing the avocets, we also had hides at a variety of other nests in the vicinity, so that during a ten-day holiday we probably photographed one dozen species, using the procedures described above with all of them.

Peter

Raoul

RED-CAPPED PLOVER, CUNNAMULLA, QUEENSLAND
Canon F1, 500mm, 1/125th sec, f4.5, Kodachrome 64

BARRED CUCKOO-SHRIKE, MOGGILL, QUEENSLAND
Pentax 200mm, 1/125th sec, f4, Ektachrome

Peter

TOWERS

Colin Lloyd called me one day to say he'd found a Barred Cuckoo-Shrike's nest. As it is one of the least-photographed common birds, I'd often mentioned to him my desire to try one. When I went around to have a look, I found out why the bird was so seldom captured on film. Forgive me for resorting to the terminology of long ago, but it sounds better to say it was 80 feet from the ground than to give the metric equivalent. Colin and I decided to hire industrial scaffolding, make a tower and hope for the best. Several days later, I was 80 feet up in the forest, with a Barred Cuckoo-Shrike sitting on its nest in front of me. The portrait I took is opposite and the tower is in the left-hand picture below. That's Colin on the platform.

Few birds place their nests at convenient heights, so it is usually necessary to use a tower, which we think of as a hide on stilts. Two more of the many towers we have used are illustrated. The central shot shows a five-metre ladder held upright by ropes and attached to a tree trunk by two lengths of timber upon which a platform is precariously balanced. Result - the kingfisher on page 18. The right-hand picture is a bush timber tower about 40 feet (twelve metres) in height, built in genuinely crocodile-infested mangroves at Point Torment, near Derby, Western Australia. That landmark is well-named, for I suffered from sandfly fever after a day in the hide trying for a picture of a Brahminy Kite.

Nowadays we use welded waterpipe sections which are bolted together *in situ*, can be erected in a few minutes and are easy to manoeuvre through the bush. It is a simple matter to lay a platform across at the appropriate height and attach a hide to it. The only hard part is shifting the tower closer once the birds have become used to it at a distance.

Peter

NANKEEN KESTREL, KELMSCOTT, WESTERN AUSTRALIA
Linhof, 270mm, 1/250th sec, f5.6, Ektachrome, Multiblitz two heads

Raoul

PACIFIC BAZA, GULUGUBA, QUEENSLAND
Mamiya RB67, 250mm, 1/125th sec, f16, Ektachrome 64, two front flashes

These two pictures were taken from two very different towers. The kestrel hide was built from scraps of building timber tied together with binder twine. The best thing I learned from several years in the Scouts was the art of lashing, or tying two bits of wood together so that they stayed together. I can't remember, but I probably failed lashing as the kestrel tower was distinctly rickety. I had to build it on one side of the nest tree, unfortunately facing into the wind, which meant that the adults landed with their backs to the camera. However, one day the wind changed for about ten minutes and I prayed that one of the kestrels would visit. Right on cue, the female flew in carrying a grasshopper, alighting in perfect position, and I got my shot.

Raoul's picture was taken from probably the most elegant tower in the world, a collapsible, portable job extending to 25 metres (80 feet), and made from aluminium. It incorporated a ladder and a winch, built by Jack and Lindsay Cupper specifically for photographing birds of prey. Jack used the tower to photograph the baza which nested at our place, and invited Raoul, who was eight years of age at the time, to try his luck. I remember standing under the ladder while Raoul disappeared skywards, wondering whether I could catch him if he fell. Jack helped him to set up the camera then left him to it and, as you can see from the picture above, some nice shots resulted.

Peter

CISTICOLA, FOGG DAM, NORTHERN TERRITORY
Canon F1, 500mm, 1/125th sec, f4.5, Kodachrome 64

Raoul

STALKING

The retaining wall of Fogg Dam near Darwin is one of the most magical places to be at sunset. Herons, egrets, ibis, ducks and geese are frantically searching for a last snack before departing to their roosts. Finches, honeyeaters and other small birds move into the open to hawk for the myriads of insects emerging in anticipation of nightfall. The Golden-headed Cisticola, opposite, hidden in the reeds for most of the day, emerges to soak up the last rays of sunlight. Walking along the dam wall with camera and tripod over one shoulder, the photographer has an endless supply of subjects. It is only a matter of moving slowly and without sudden gestures, manoeuvring to keep partly hidden behind a bush, ready to set the tripod down and rapidly focus, enjoying the primeval urge to hunt without the traditional bloody conclusion. While Fogg Dam may be the ultimate in stalking localities, there are few places where at least some birds cannot be found, even if they are "only" sparrows. Even the back garden can be productive (see pages 88, 112, 120 and 152). Usually birds in towns are tamer than bush birds (pages 156-7).

Stalking for birds is dependent on using a long lens and a sturdy tripod. The longer the lens the better, because it means one doesn't have to get quite so close. Even so, much persistence is needed to close the gap, selectivity is required to wait for the pleasing composition and anticipation, based on knowledge of the species, helps the photographer to out-think the bird and be ready for its next move. Handy hints are not to move straight towards a bird but zig-zag at an angle, to look out of the corners of the eyes rather than directly at the subject and not to stop or start suddenly.

Some photographers use tape-recorders to call birds close but it is a method we prefer not to use, because it provokes unnatural behaviour and, if used near a nest, can cause unnecessary and unforgivable distress to the parent birds.

"Stalking" in a boat is particularly effective for waterbirds, as the human silhouette is not so obvious, and one can approach much closer than on foot.

Peter

PIED HERON IN SUNSHOWER, MIDDLE POINT, NORTHERN TERRITORY
Canon F1, 500mm, 1.4 teleconverter (= 700mm), 1/125th sec, f6.3, Ektachrome Elite 400

SPOTTED BOWERBIRD AND THE TUNNEL OF LOVE, CUNNAMULLA, QUEENSLAND

Raoul

Hasselblad ELM, 250mm, 25mm extension tube, 1/125th sec, f11, Fujichrome 100, two fill-in flashes and a toplight flash over bower

MY FAVOURITE PHOTOGRAPHS

I love birds for their freedom. Without effort, they can fly anywhere. I am drawn to their flight and imagine looking through their eyes. Caged birds, with all their bright colours, do nothing to excite me.

A photograph of a wild bird implies trust. The bird has a choice between allowing me close enough to photograph it and escaping. I have appreciated the confidence birds have given me and I have tried to repay them by making pictures of them full of joy and lightness.

The process of photographing also interests me. In a world full of technological marvels, photography seems to me to be the one closest to magic. I have found that the harder I work with the camera, the more magical are the rewards.

My two favourites among the photographs I have taken are shown here. The rooster was my debut effort and, as in all things, the first time is special. Also, I feel that it is a damn fine effort for a seven-year-old, barefooted boy on a frosty morning. There were always loaded cameras lying around our home and even at that age I was encouraged to use them.

The Spotted Bowerbird is special to me because it encapsulates everything that I feel is important for a successful bird photo. The bird looks beautiful, like a model, and is caught in an unusual pose in sympathetic light. Less obvious is the essential hand of luck that underpowered my fill-in flashes, resulting in the dramatic dominance of the toplight. All of the other shots taken at this bower (about 60 in all) were more evenly lit; I probably took this one before the flash lights had fully recharged - it was the one picture in the series that would have most benefited from the resulting lighting effect. I look at this photo and smile at the good fortune that helped me, and has led me close to so many other birds.

Raoul

GREAT EGRET, LAKE TOOLIBIN, WESTERN AUSTRALIA
Praktisix, 180mm, 1/25th sec, f5.6, Ektachrome, Multiblitz two heads

MY FAVOURITE PHOTOGRAPH

My first bird pictures were made with a folding Brownie camera in the nineteen forties. I was advised to stand with my back to the sun and take pictures only between the hours of nine a.m. and four p.m., when the light was deemed to be bright enough. Nowadays most of my pictures are taken outside those parameters, in early morning and evening light looking towards the sun.

The picture opposite was responsible for a change in my approach from a photographer basically committed to sharp, well-lit close-ups aimed at the most ornithologically accurate representation of the bird to one interested in more personal and, hopefully, artistic interpretations. I suppose it led ultimately to phasing out photography and taking up painting.

We put up a hide near the egret colony at Lake Toolibin, Western Australia, to watch, not photograph, the nesting birds. When we returned later, two pairs of egrets had begun building in the tree supporting the hide, so we reasoned it would be churlish not to take a few pictures of them.

While watching, I was entranced by the plumes raised in display and for no reason I can specifically remember decided that they would look best lit from behind. So on my next visit I placed my flashes well behind the nest, allowing just a kiss of light to fall on the bird. For the plan to work the picture had to be dark, so I underexposed. Most of the shots of the egrets displaying failed for one reason or another, but towards evening, when the sky was turning red, the egret began preening - as I pressed the shutter I knew this was the one. For once my mental picture was matched by the image on film.

Peter

PALM COCKATOO, LOCKHART RIVER, QUEENSLAND
Canon F1, 500mm, 1/60th sec, f4.5, Kodachrome 200

All birds have character. Even the most timid have a certain presence. Others have attitude in spades. All of the individuals of the one species tend to be alike; all Magpie Larks are feisty, all Corellas are larrikins, all Willie Wagtails give you their opinion without being asked. Emus and Palm Cockatoos are two of my favourites and with these photos I've tried to show a little of their essence.

The emu looks to me like a foolish bird trying to be dignified. Its movements are stately, yet its wild, unkempt hairstyle, mad eyes and bizarre toothed beak reveal the species' inner giddiness. To attract this bird, I lay on my back and pedalled my legs (and I call the emu foolish!). The bird came rushing up, an awesome sight from my supine position, and gaped curiously at the camera.

The Palm Cockatoo is a ruffian's bird. With its immense crest, red eyepatch and cutlass of a beak, it is an ally any pirate would be proud to have perched on his shoulder.

Raoul

Raoul

EMU, TUMBLING WATERS, NORTHERN TERRITORY
Canon F1, 500mm, 1/125th sec, f4.5, Ektachrome Elite 100

AUSTRALASIAN GREBE, BRISBANE, QUEENSLAND
Hasselblad ELM, 250 mm, 1/125th sec, f8/11, Ektachrome 64, two front flashes and backlight flash

Raoul

When I was a youngster, my favourite bird was the Australasian Grebe. My first sight of it was on a small lake where a number of pairs fought for territory by running across the surface of the water while crying out challenges. This ferocity was an intriguing counterpoint to their cuddly-toy appearance. At that stage of my life, I imagined having a pet guard-grebe, that would mind my swimming pool by day then, suitably dried-off, keep my feet warm at night. As an adolescent, I wanted a grebe hairstyle for myself - black coif, chestnut temples and yellow sideburns. Sadly, the hairdresser declined the challenge.

Raoul

GREAT CRESTED GREBE, WOODANILLING, WESTERN AUSTRALIA
Hasselblad ELM, 1/250th sec, f8, Fujichrome 100, two front flashes

Grebes are fascinating birds and I have spent many happy hours in hides watching them. A bird attending its nest is always in motion, adjusting the floating platform, fanning the eggs to cool them or snapping at dragonflies daring enough to perch nearby. In the picture opposite, the chicks have just hatched out and are taking shelter with their mother as a heavy storm brews. I am particularly fascinated by the sexually charged pyrotechnics of the Great Crested Grebe displays (such as the "cat" display shown here), an attraction shared by many birdwatchers, most notably Julian Huxley, who made them the subject of the first serious study of bird behaviour.

Raoul

BLACK SWAN AND SURFER, HEALESVILLE, VICTORIA, AND CAIRNS, QUEENSLAND

Swan: Canon F1, 500mm, 1/125th sec, f4.5; Surfer: Canon AE1, 50mm, 1/250th, f5.6

Raoul

Raoul

BLACK SWAN HEAD, HEALESVILLE, VICTORIA
Canon F1, 500mm, 125th sec, f4.5

Bird watching and photography are two very fickle pursuits. Bring them together and the odds multiply and stack against you: the bird flies away, the camera breaks down, the weather turns bad, the film is scratched. When roll after roll of film goes into the bin, you can begin to believe that the only luck possible is bad.

The photo of the Black Swan and the Surfer is the good luck that cancels out all the bad luck I've ever had. I'd taken a few shots of a surfer at sunset, wound the film out of the camera and forgot about it. After a couple of years, I re-exposed the roll with moody, dark shots of swans. Somehow, two frames registered perfectly and the exposures added well. All the other double exposures didn't work but this one did. Sometimes luck smiles.

The other swan portrait is from the same roll. I was after the feel of a swan gliding silently in the water. Foliage separated me from the bird, but I shot anyway, knowing that with a long lens at its widest aperture the leaves would blur and add the right softness to the photo.

Raoul

FOLLOWING PAGES:
SOFTLY, SOFTLY, BLACK SWANS, LAKE MANCHESTER, QUEENSLAND (*Raoul*)
Linhof Technika 67, Rotelar 270mm, 1/10th sec, f22, Fujichrome 50

PAINTED SNIPE, MUNKEJARRA, NEAR DERBY, WESTERN AUSTRALIA
Pentax, 400mm, 1/125th sec, f8, Kodachrome 25

Peter

Painted Snipe are such elusive birds that it is difficult to judge whether they are genuinely rare or just hard to find. However, I have been lucky enough to come across quite a few, usually by accident when looking for something else. At Munkejarra Waterhole I found a number of nests one Wet season, the first time Painted Snipe had been recorded nesting in the West. When I first found the nests, the owners had slipped away undetected and it was not until I put up a hide and sat in it several days later that I found out they were Painted Snipe.

My picture is of a male bird incubating in a clump of samphire. The male looks after the eggs and young and is more plainly coloured than the polyandrous female – she is a beautiful creature, but no matter how hard I tried I could not get close enough to her for a decent picture. Judging by the experience at Munkejarra, she takes up to four mates, as the nests I found were localised in groups of three or four. Only one nest was in samphire, the rest being hidden by clumps of grass, where the longitudinal stripes on the males' plumage perfectly matched bent blades of grass, effectively hiding the birds from view.

Peter

BLACK-FRONTED DOTTEREL, GULUGUBA, QUEENSLAND
No technical data recorded

The first birds I photographed were nesting in summer at a dam near Kalgoorlie, Western Australia - one was a kingfisher and the other was a dotterel. I cannot remember which was first, but I do remember tying my mother's folding Brownie camera to a stake driven into the ground about half a metre from the dotterel's eggs, attaching a long string to the shutter release and retreating to await the bird's return. I recall my breathless anticipation as the dotterel circled about summoning enough courage to face the camera. At last she ran straight to the nest and squatted down over her eggs; I gently pulled the string and the direction my life was to take for the next twenty years was determined.

My father showed the resulting photograph to his friend, Bishop Elsey of Kalgoorlie, who gave me a book from his library. It was written and illustrated at the turn of the century by the Kearton brothers concerning their innovative contribution to the art of bird photography, namely the construction and use of hides. Remembering the dotterels' hesitations, I was convinced by the Keartons' arguments, and used hides from then on for photography at nests. This picture is similar to that first effort, but it is even nearer to my heart because it was taken at a nest found by my father, Sam, on his last visit to us.

Peter

47

BLACK-FRONTED DOTTEREL, CUNNAMULLA, QUEENSLAND

Raoul

Hasselblad ELM, 250mm + 25mm extension, 1/125th sec, f11, Ektachrome 64, two front flashes

To be effective, a hide should have just two small holes. The camera lens fits through one and above that is a viewing hole. As you can imagine, the hide becomes stifling on hot days and the view can become very tedious if nothing is happening. Many hours I have spent cramped in hides sweating and killing time with mental games. In fact, if I had to describe myself I would emphasise three characteristics which are probably due to all the time I've spent in hides - stooped, thin and difficult to bore.

Raoul

RED-NECKED AVOCETS CHANGING OVER NEST DUTY, CUNNAMULLA, QUEENSLAND
Hasselblad ELM, 250mm, 1/250th sec, f11, Fujichrome 100, two front flashes, natural backlight

There is an enormous temptation to take a book into a hide, but this is counter-productive. Birds are very secretive around their nests and come and go silently while the pages are being turned. There may only be a few opportunities in the course of a day to photograph and even fewer in which something happens to lift a photograph out of the ordinary. If concentration is lost, one ends up with a roll of 'stuffed' birds sitting side-on to the camera like duck cutouts in a shooting gallery. The extraordinary moment, as when the bird stands over its eggs, or when both birds come to the nest together, is worth waiting for.

Raoul

BANDED PLOVER, CUNNAMULLA, QUEENSLAND
Canon F1, 500mm, 1/125th sec, f4.5, Kodachrome 64

Raoul

This picture resulted from the ultimate in serendipity. We particularly wanted to locate a Banded Plover's nest to photograph on a trip to our favourite spot near Cunnamulla, on Blairmore Station. There were plenty of plovers around and we spent several days watching them in the mulga, hoping to be led to a suitable site. Eventually we gave up, assuming that they had finished nesting. We moved camp a kilometre or so, and while setting up saw some plovers off in the distance. I had been watching them through binoculars for half an hour or so when I became aware of an out-of-focus blob in the foreground. As I refocused, it resolved into a plover sitting on its nest in a clump of daisies, about 30 metres away from our camp. Normally one can't get within half a kilometre of a nest without the owner slipping away unobserved. My picture was taken a few days later in early morning light, looking directly into the sun but, unlike the situation opposite, lens flare would have detracted from the result, so an extra long lens hood was used, creating a totally different effect.

Raoul

PELICAN AND GULLS, BROOMSHEAD, NEW SOUTH WALES
Canon AE1, 100-300mm zoom, 1/500th sec, f8, Kodachrome 64

I particularly like using lens flare to simplify and warm a photo. The sun shining directly into a lens will cause the glass elements to light up. In a wide-angle lens this leads to an unpleasant line of bright rings and partial clouding. The results with a telephoto are much more pleasing, causing the whole photo to soften and take on the lustre of the light.

The gulls looked comically like spectators at a pelican sporting event, so I focused on them rather than on the foreground. Usually it is best to focus on the nearest subject, but in this case I feel the exception works.

Raoul

SHAGGY DOG - LITTLE PIED CORMORANT SHAKES ITSELF DRY, KANGAROO GULLY, QUEENSLAND
Canon AE1, 100-300mm zoom, 1/30th sec, f8, Kodachrome 64

Raoul

Raoul   PLUCKED (CATTLE EGRET PREENING), KANGAROO GULLY, QUEENSLAND
Canon AE1, 100-300mm, 1/125th sec, f5.6, Kodachrome 64

A Cattle Egret colony first attracted me to this dam. The birds started drifting in to roost about an hour before sunset and would spend some time drinking and preening at a partially submerged tree before finding a place to sleep. I set a hide on the bank near the tree so that it faced into the setting sun. For a few days, only Cattle Egrets came, and I was lucky enough to have the camera trained on this individual when it plucked a feather from its side.

On one occasion a flock of Cormorants swam past. Cormorants lack the waterproofing of most birds, so their saturated feathers caused them to float very low. One by one they jumped up onto perches and shook themselves dry. I visualised a photo with the backlit droplets cutting a halo of streaks around the bird and set the camera on a slow shutter speed, 1/30th, to capture that effect.

Raoul

BUSH STONE-CURLEW   *Peter*
Hasselblad, 250mm, 1/250th sec, f5.6, Ektachrome, two front flashes, one backlight

A pair of stone-curlews nested over a period of time on the property of Mrs Grieves at Kenmore, Queensland. She was justifiably proud of them and let me know each year when the eggs were laid. I was hoping for a picture of an adult with its chicks just after hatching, but for two years missed out. On the third year, I arrived early in the morning just as the chicks were about to leave the nest. We had put up a hide in anticipation, so I hurriedly set up inside and waited for the brooding bird to relax from her "broken stick" attitude. Suddenly she decided all was well and fluffed out her feathers, changing shape completely, looking much more beautiful. I had a few minutes to take my shots before she stood and led the chicks off into the forest.

Peter

MASKED PLOVER, ANSTEAD, QUEENSLAND
Hasselblad, 500mm, 1/125th sec, f8, Ektachrome

This is what passes for lawn at our place, not very aesthetic but good for birds. The plover in the photo and its mate nest two or three times each year at the same time as half a dozen other pairs in our valley. Usually after they have been incubated for three or four days the eggs of all pairs are taken on the same night by a fox, but occasionally one or two pairs manage to hatch their chicks. This shot was taken in our backyard while the chicks were drying out after emerging, the best time to photograph ground-nesting birds provided a hide is carefully set up well in advance. By using a long tele-lens, a close approach is avoided, minimising any disturbance to the birds.

Peter

INTERMEDIATE EGRET, OLD JIM JIM HIGHWAY, NORTHERN TERRITORY

Canon F1, 500mm, 1/1000th sec, f11, Ektachrome Elite 100

Raoul

Looking into the sun as it is reflected off water can offer some interesting photographic possibilities. The only other time when there is such an amount of light available for fast shutter speeds is at noon on clear days, and that lighting is too harsh and unpleasant for photography.

These photos show two ways in which reflections may be used. The frozen action in both highlights the shutter speed possible. The exposure above was taken from the egret, so that it carries detail while the reflections which were brighter have burnt out into white. The landscape at Anbangbang (opposite) was cluttered and untidy, with a boring foreground and background, so I exposed for the water, knowing this would turn everything else into silhouettes and simplify the composition. Film lacks the range to show detail in both the water and the subject unless the sunlight is softened by cloud or a low angle in the sky.

Raoul

Raoul

MAGPIE GEESE, ANBANGBANG BILLABONG, NORTHERN TERRITORY
Canon F1, 500mm, 1/1000th sec, f16, Kodachrome 64

NANKEEN NIGHT-HERON, LAKE TOOLIBIN, WESTERN AUSTRALIA
Linhof, 270mm, 1/125th sec, f8, Ektachrome, Multiblitz two heads

Peter

Peter

RED-NECKED AVOCET, LAKE BIDDY, WESTERN AUSTRALIA
Linhof, 270mm, 1/125th sec, f5.6, Ektachrome 64

Night-herons nested in loose colonies among the casuarinas near the famous egret colony on Lake Toolibin. We set up near one nest, not hoping for much activity due to the birds' nocturnal habits. However, I found that they behaved much like diurnal herons, even feeding their chicks during the afternoon and displaying their three white plumes in spectacular greeting ceremonies. Alas, I inadvertently left the dark slide in the camera for most of the day, so I missed recording all the best action.

Several hundred kilometres due east of the freshwater Lake Toolibin lies a series of salt pans linked to Lake Biddy. When they hold water they attract many birds, for they teem with brine shrimps. Avocets, stilts and dotterels nest on islands and I spent many happy hours with Ray Garstone and Walter Keighley taking pictures. This is my favourite, taken from a hide after a thunderstorm, when the light was exquisite.

Peter

59

PIED HERON, RED LILY LAGOON, KAKADU, NORTHERN TERRITORY
Nikon F90, 300mm + 1.4 extender, auto-exposure at f5.6, Ektachrome 100

Peter

Raoul

PIED HERON AND LITTLE EGRET, FOGG DAM, NORTHERN TERRITORY
Canon F1, 500mm, 1/250th sec, f5.6, Kodachrome 200

We spent several productive days off the beaten track at Red Lily Lagoon in Kakadu National Park early in August. When we arrived, we sat for an hour just watching to see if any patterns of bird movements were obvious. After a while, we noticed one corner which herons and egrets visited often, so set up a hide there. While I was photographing one morning, a crocodile emerged about five metres away and slid up onto the mud bank. I sat quite still for several hours. The birds paid no attention, in fact, most of them went out of their way to have a good look at the reptile. Of my results, I liked the Pied Heron opposite best. Raoul likes more action in his shots, so he picked the interaction above, taken while stalking at Fogg Dam.

Peter

WHITE-NECKED HERON, CUNNAMULLA, QUEENSLAND
Canon F1, 500mm, 1/250th sec, f5.6, Kodachrome 64

Raoul

Usually swaying high up in a tower makes me feel a trifle uneasy, but on this occasion I was glad to be up there. The heron nest was in a swamp out in mulga country. While photographing, I heard a sound like a herd of horses galloping through the water. A peek from the hide revealed an enormous feral pig powering along like a landing barge. The length of its body was out of proportion to its legs, so that it was the size and shape of a dining table. I didn't move or breathe until it was well out of view. The herons proved to be absorbing subjects, with beautiful colouring which includes rich russets and subtle grey-blues. One adult kept me entertained with a long display performed with a branch that it broke off. The photo was taken as the bird overbalanced slightly while descending to the nest to care for its tiny chick.

Raoul

GREAT EGRET, LAKE TOOLIBIN, WESTERN AUSTRALIA (*Peter*)
Linhof 5x4, 270mm, 1/125th sec, f11, two front flashlights

GREAT EGRET, LAKE TOOLIBIN, WESTERN AUSTRALIA
Praktisix, 180mm, 1/125th sec, f5.6, Ektachrome

Peter

Raoul

LITTLE EGRETS AND PIED HERON, FOGG DAM, NORTHERN TERRITORY
Canon F1, 500mm, 1/8th sec, f16, Ektachrome Elite 100

When we put up a hide about 50 metres from the egret heronry on Lake Toolibin we were expecting to watch behaviour, not to photograph, but unexpectedly two pairs built alongside the hide, so whenever I attended I used two cameras, one focused on each nest. It is hard to imagine that the picture on the facing page was taken only a few metres away from that on page 36. Because of their aspects and backgrounds, they look totally different. I sometimes use the two shots in talks to illustrate the difference between "low key" and "high key"; this one epitomises the latter. It was only possible because the sun was obscured by heavy cloud, resulting in soft, even light. Similar light made Raoul's picture work - he used a very slow shutter speed to emphasise the action.

Peter

GREAT EGRET, FOGG DAM, NORTHERN TERRITORY *Raoul*
Canon AE1, 500mm, 1/250th sec, f4.5, Kodachrome 200

Raoul

GREAT EGRET STRIKING, FOGG DAM, NORTHERN TERRITORY
Canon AEI, 500mm + 1.4 extender (= 700mm), 1/250th sec, f4.5, Kodachrome 200

The pleasure that is derived from looking at a photo or a painting doesn't necessarily come from appreciating the subject as a whole. The subject may be perceived as a combination of abstract lines, shapes, textures, colours, tones, sizes or directions. The way these elements inter-relate and contrast can form pleasing compositions and I am always searching out strong design elements in nature for my photos.

The shape of an egret is one of my favourites. This bird's sinuous, lean curves are the definition of elegance. During breeding, sprays of plumes soften their severe outlines. The result is a magical design: shape, line, contrast and repetitive harmony. Such beauty could only come in pure white.

My main interest in these two egrets was their elongated shape. Taking the photo on the left, I had the eerie experience of being fixed by the egret's unflinching gaze. I had to laugh; where does the egret keep its brain? When taking the right-hand photo, I watched the egret fish in a small pool as the sun set. He held his head over to one side, presumably creating an angle that hid him from the fish. Then, with a lightning stroke so smooth that it didn't leave a ripple, he speared his head into the water. I like the undisturbed water, and the way the bird's odd shape is repeated by its reflection.

Raoul

CROCODILE AND JABIRU REFLECTION, YELLOW WATERS, NORTHERN TERRITORY
Canon F1, 500mm, 1/500th sec, f5.6, Kodachrome 64

Raoul

Raoul

HOARY-HEADED GREBE IN NARDOO, CUNNAMULLA, QUEENSLAND
Hasselblad ELM, 250mm, 1/125th sec, f11, Ektachrome 64, two frontlights and one backlight

The best place in Australia for photographing birds is mulga woodland after a wet winter. Nothing matches it for birds, it dazzles the eye with a carpet of yellow wildflowers and the air is heavy with their fragrance. You can never grow used to that scent, as shifting winds bring subtle changes from the different species around. One sight will never leave me, that of a salt pan covered in Nardoo lily, like hectares of bright yellow silk unrolled in the mulga. That incomparable sight exists for maybe two months in every ten years and I count myself lucky to have been a witness to it. We camped at this spot for a fortnight, photographing grebes, wrens, woodswallows, bowerbirds and chats among the yellow flowers. I remember feeling a quiet regret for the bouquet I crushed with each step.

Raoul

SPLENDID FAIRY-WREN, CUNNAMULLA, QUEENSLAND (*Raoul*)
Hasselblad ELM, 250mm + 50mm extension tube, 1/60th sec, f8/11, Ektachrome, two frontlights and one backlight

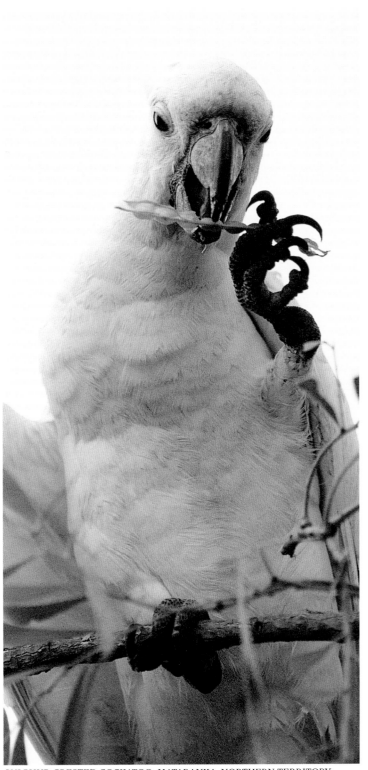

SULPHUR-CRESTED COCKATOO, MATARANKA, NORTHERN TERRITORY
Canon F1, 500mm, 1/125th sec, f4.5, Kodachrome 64

LITTLE CORELLA, COOINDA, NORTHERN TERRITORY
Canon F1, 500mm, 1/60th sec, f4.5, Kodachrome 64

Raoul

LITTLE CORELLAS PLAY-FIGHTING, SOUTH ALLIGATOR RIVER, NORTHERN TERRITORY
Canon F1, 500mm, 1/250th sec, f4.5, Ektachrome Elite 400

Try telling me that birds don't play, or that they don't have a sense of humour. Sure, there are some little dull brown jobs like the scrubwrens that work in the accounts department of the bird world, but most feathered creatures are infused with a tremendous zest for life. The cockatoos in particular not only act joyfully but seem to smile right back at you.

Raoul

LITTLE EGRET, FOGG DAM, NORTHERN TERRITORY
Canon F1, 500mm, 1/15th sec, f4.5, Ektachrome Elite 100

Raoul

In 1992, Broken Hill suffered an invasion of Corellas. By day they fed at the cattle lots and each evening they swarmed in thousands into the cemetery. There they stripped the trees bare, pulled the flowers from the graves and played havoc with the overhead wires. I took to driving through the graveyard looking for photos, but the birds only arrived after dark. When I lined up this photo the camera told me to use 1/8th second. I knew from experience that anything taken from the car window slower than 1/30th second would come out blurred. The name "Cyril" caught my eye, so I took a shot anyway at 1/30th, the slowest speed possible. As a result the photo is dark and the birds and headstones seem to glow from within.

The Little Egret was also taken in marginal light. The sun broke through a storm for a few seconds and lit this Egret ruffling its plumes. Just one feather on its back stands out and this makes the photo for me.

Raoul

Raoul

"CYRIL" AND THE CORELLAS, BROKEN HILL, NEW SOUTH WALES
Canon F1, 500mm, 1/30th sec, f4.5, Kodachrome 64

GALAHS, MATARANKA, NORTHERN TERRITORY
Canon F1, 500mm, 1/125th sec, f4.5, Kodachrome 200

Raoul

Mataranka thermal hot springs form an oasis in an expanse of dry eucalypt savannah. I always keep an eye out for this sort of sudden change in the landscape or vegetation, because this is where wildlife seems to concentrate. Mataranka is known for its flying-fox colony, which can number a quarter of a million individuals. Great Bowerbirds and Shining Flycatchers, two of my favourite birds, are also common there.

One morning, I rose early and went stalking for quail in a horse paddock close to the springs. A flock of Galahs landed close by, interested in drinking at a horse trough. I had seen Galahs watering before and knew that they held their wings open for a second after alighting. I pictured them lined up along the trough in that pose and set the camera about 12 metres away from the trough, looking into the sunrise. The process of recognising an opportunity and working out how to achieve the image is very pleasurable. The Galahs didn't seem concerned by my closeness. They descended and began drinking and squabbling. The northern version of the Galah is a faded pink, looking as if it has been through the washing machine once too often. The pastel colours suit the soft light in these photos.

Raoul

Raoul

GALAHS, MATARANKA, NORTHERN TERRITORY
Canon F1, 500mm, 125th sec, f4.5, Kodachrome 200

FOLLOWING PAGES:
GALAH FEATHER, SILVERTON, NEW SOUTH WALES (*Raoul*)
Linhof Technika 67, Rodenstock 135mm, 81A warming filter, 1 sec, f45, Fujichrome 100

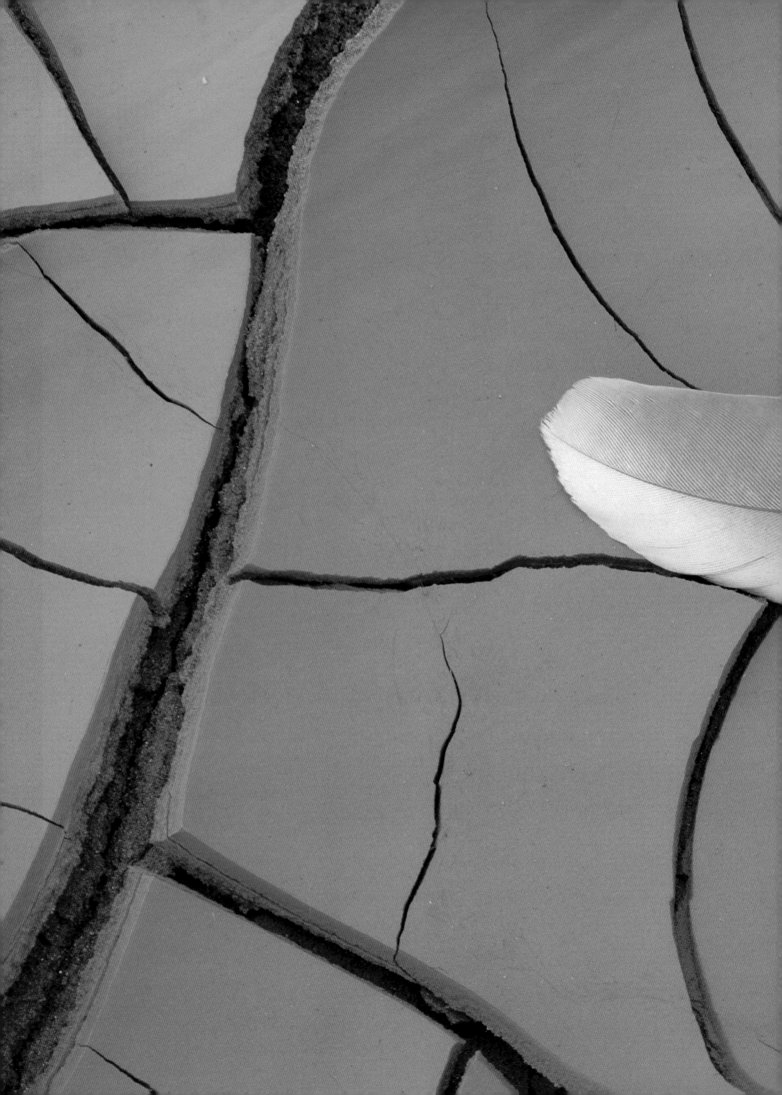

Raoul

CRIMSON ROSELLA, BINNA BURRA, QUEENSLAND
Canon F1, 500mm, 1/60th sec, f4.5, Kodachrome 64

A pair of Pale-headed Rosellas had been visiting the garden and performing the tail-shaking display that precedes nesting. In response, my father and I wired a number of hollow logs into trees. Within an hour, the rosellas were investigating the hollows. By the next day, they had decided on their favourite. We set up a tower and I photographed them at the nest before eggs were laid. This is a rewarding practice with parrots, as they spend a lot of time early on at the entrance to the hollow, displaying, grooming and sunning. After the eggs are laid, the birds are at the entrance for only moments each day until the chicks are big enough to emerge to be fed.

The photo shows an unusual display. The adult presses the bare skin over its beak to all parts of the potential nest site. I assume this is to gauge the temperature and therefore the suitability of the hollow for nesting.

Raoul

PALE-HEADED ROSELLA, BRISBANE, QUEENSLAND (*Raoul*)
Mamiya RB67, 360mm, 1/60th sec, f11, Fuji 100, two front flashes

81

RED-COLLARED LORIKEETS, NOONAMAH, NORTHERN TERRITORY *Raoul*
Canon F1, 500mm, 1/125th sec, f4.5, Ektachrome Elite 400

Look no further than the garden. There is enough nature in the back yard to photograph for a year. Particularly in those parts of Australia that show the effect of the seasons, a procession of wildlife will pass the door. When I don't have time to travel, I will go hunting for insects with a macro lens in the local park or nature reserve. Birds are attracted into the centre of cities by flowering garden plants, and when driving around I watch out for this. I even considered renting a unit for a week because its verandah overlooked a tree frequented by parrots.

Raoul

SCALY-BREASTED LORIKEETS, BRISBANE, QUEENSLAND
Hasselblad ELM, 250mm + 25mm extension tube, 1/125th sec, f8, Fujichrome, two front flashes

These lorikeets were photographed in friends' backyards. The Red-collareds came daily to a feeder. The best time to photograph was before food was put out, because the lorikeets sat around expectantly and displayed to each other. Once there was food, there was chaos! The Scaly-breasteds were taken from a tower set near an Umbrella tree. The lorikeets in Brisbane are very tame, so I didn't need a hide. I particularly like this photo because the compositional elements come together in a really pleasing way.

Raoul

RED-TAILED BLACK-COCKATOOS, JIM JIM HIGHWAY, NORTHERN TERRITORY
Canon F1, 500mm + 1.4 teleconverter (= 700mm), 1/125th sec, f4.5, Ektachrome Elite 400

CORELLA SENTINEL   *Peter*
Nikon F90, 300mm, auto-exposure at f4, Fujichrome 400

Cockatoos are birds that are most often seen in flocks, and are generally difficult to approach because one or two wary individuals keep a watch-out, acting more or less as sentinels. I like to think the corella in the lower shot is such a sentinel uttering a warning. Certainly I was well hidden and the picture was taken as some people approached along the wall at Fogg Dam.

The budgerigars were at the entrance to their nest hollow, about 50 centimetres from the ground as indicated by the wildflowers in the corner. In the same tree, which was only five metres high, half a dozen more pairs, as well as some Tree Martins, were nesting. The martins constantly dive-bombed the budgerigars, probably assuming that they wanted to usurp their hollow.

Peter

Peter

BUDGERIGAR PAIR AT NEST HOLLOW
Nikon F90, 300mm, auto-exposure at f4, Ektachrome 100

BUDGERIGARS, MURCHISON RIVER, WESTERN AUSTRALIA
Nikon F90, 300mm, auto-exposure at f4, Ektachrome 100

Peter

I have spent a lot of time studying the Budgerigar, as I feel that it is the essentially Australian bird. It occurs in enormous numbers when conditions in the interior are favourable. These shots were taken in a river gum on the Murchison River – from one position, I had half a dozen nest hollows within camera range, one less than a metre from the ground. The male in the picture above, preening his mate after feeding her, was also feeding another female at a nest ten metres away. One female had seven eggs, the other six, and they probably had three broods each while conditions were right, so this male potentially added nearly 40 chicks to the population in one season. Budgerigars are good photographic subjects. Provided you stay still and use a reasonably long lens, they continue their frenetic existence as if you were not there. I have even had one land on me while I was filling a billy at a waterhole in the desert.

Peter

Peter

BUDGERIGAR, MURCHISON RIVER, WESTERN AUSTRALIA
Nikon F90, 300mm, auto-exposure at f4, Ektachrome 100

TAWNY FROGMOUTH AND CHICKS, KANGAROO GULLY, QUEENSLAND
Mamiya RB67, 250mm, 1/500th sec, f11, Fujichrome 100, two front flashes

Peter

A pair of frogmouths has frequented our garden for many years and has become quite tame. Each Spring, they perch in the same tree with their chicks, usually on the same branch which matches their plumage so well. Once the chicks are well grown, they disappear and we don't see them again – the adults don't use that tree again until the following year's chicks are fledged.

Peter

TAWNY FROGMOUTH WINKING, KANGAROO GULLY, QUEENSLAND (*Raoul*)
Hasselblad ELM, 250mm, 1/125th sec, f5.6, Ektachrome 64, two front flashes

BARKING OWL WITH JACANA, FOGG DAM, NORTHERN TERRITORY
Nikon F90, 300mm, auto-exposure and auto-focus with SB-25 flash, Fujichrome 100

Peter

We spent several nights at Fogg Dam photographing Barking Owls. As one used to manually adjusted equipment, I found my newly acquired Nikon F90 and SB-25 flash miraculous. The flash sits on top of the camera and throws a narrow red beam, which automatically focuses the lens. All we had to do was find an owl, spotlight it with the beam and press the shutter. The flash even pre-fires a pulse of light which eliminates the red reflection in the owl's eyes. We saw this owl from the car window while we were driving along the dam wall, leaned out and took three or four shots before realising it was feeding on a jacana, which it must have plucked from a lily-pad after dark.

Peter

Raoul

ADULT BARKING OWL, SHADY CAMP, NORTHERN TERRITORY
Canon F1, 500mm + 1.4 teleconverter (= 700mm), 1/60th sec, f6.3, Ektachrome Elite 400

BARN OWL, NEAR DERBY, WESTERN AUSTRALIA
Pentax, 135mm, 1/60th sec, f16, Kodachrome 64, Multiblitz two heads

I photographed several Barn Owls while we were living in Derby many years ago. I think this one was a solitary bird that lived in a Boab hollow near the Fitzroy River flood plain. She laid eggs every year but they were infertile. I don't think she had a mate as we never saw another bird with her. She always flew straight into her hollow without pausing at the entrance, so the only way to photograph her was when she landed in the tree. I used a torch with a red filter to help focusing at night, which is only marginally better than focusing in darkness.

Peter

While setting up camp under the circus-tent-sized fig tree at Shady Camp, I had a prickly feeling I was being watched and looked up. Directly overhead was a Barking Owl chick (opposite), who was very interested in my toiling. A further search of the tree revealed the parents, one of which is shown on page 91. Daytime is their sleep period, so they were very relaxed about being photographed.

Raoul

92

Raoul

BARKING OWL CHICK, SHADY CAMP, NORTHERN TERRITORY
Canon F1, 500mm, 1/250th sec, f4.5, Kodachrome 200

Peter

WILLY WAGTAIL HARASSING LITTLE EAGLE , WOODANILLING, WESTERN AUSTRALIA
Praktisix, 180mm, 1/25th sec, f11, Ektachrome 64, Multiblitz two heads

The Little Eagle usually nests quite high in inaccessible trees but I have managed to photograph a few, some with help from friends. Ray Garstone found this one and Ken Else helped us put up the hide. I don't think Ken had climbed a tree before, but he was fearless. My heart almost stopped when I saw him hanging by one hand while arranging some ropes with the other some 25 metres above the ground. While I was in the hide one day, a violent storm blew up and the tree whipped alarmingly in the wind. I expected the branch to break at any moment but couldn't get out of the hide because the eagle was sheltering her chick. An hour earlier I had taken the shot of the wagtail on the eagle's back and I can remember thinking that if the tree went at least I could die happy. Ken probably wouldn't even have noticed the danger.

Peter

LITTLE EAGLE, WOODANILLING, WESTERN AUSTRALIA (*Peter*)
Praktisix, 180mm, 1/25th sec, f11, Ektachrome 64, Multiblitz two heads

BLACK KITE, ANNABURROO BILLABONG, NORTHERN TERRITORY
Canon F1, 500mm + 1.4 x converter (= 700mm), 1/125th sec, f6.3, Ektachrome Elite 100

Raoul

I like the danger that photography sometimes brings. Jumping from branch to branch high up in a eucalypt, holding on to a swaying tower in a willy-willy, or scrabbling up a cliff for a clear view of a landscape can all bring a feeling of being alive. Even better is the knowledge that I love doing something so much that it can drive me to do dangerous things. Too much time is spent living without passion.

This is my best effort so far at showing a kite in a bushfire. These masters of flight gather in their hundreds at the edge of burns to catch the insects trying to escape. Flames, smoke, heat and the "rip" of burning spear grass make this a dramatic spectacle. At first, I tried to photograph the action with a wide-angle, jumping through the flames to shoot from the burnt side. The air was so hot that I feared that the film would melt. On later attempts, I used a short telephoto, but shifting winds nearly choked me. The safest alternative has proved to be a long lens, although the greater amount of smoke between the subject and camera degrades the image. Here the fire was on the other side of a billabong, but even then the noise and heat were oppressive.

Raoul

FEMALE OSPREY WITH CHICKS, THEVENARD ISLAND, WESTERN AUSTRALIA (*Peter*)
Praktisix, 180mm, 1/125th sec, f8, Ektachrome

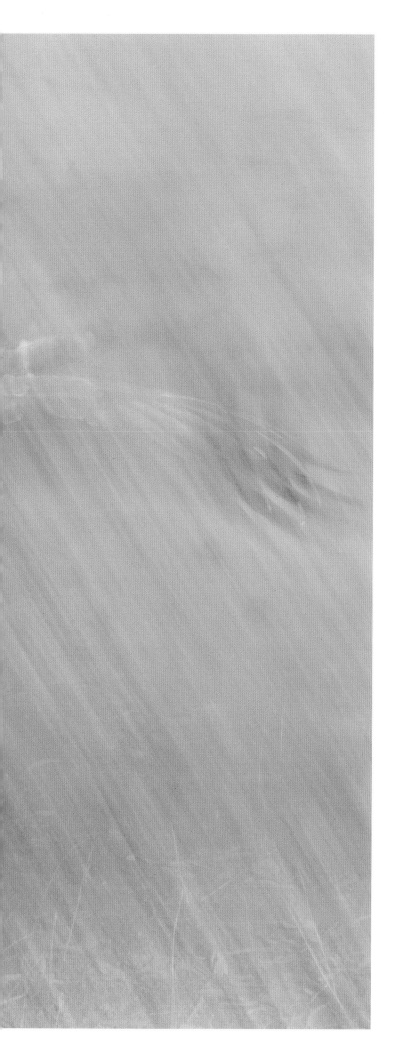

Silently passing

leaving only the imprint

of wings on the wind

Peter

SQUARE-TAILED KITE, KATANNING, WESTERN AUSTRALIA (*Peter*)
Praktisix, 300mm, 1/25th sec, f8, Ektachrome

SQUARE-TAILED KITE MANTLING, DRYANDRA, WESTERN AUSTRALIA

Raoul

Hasselblad ELM, 250mm, 1/125th sec, f8, Ektachrome 64, two front flashes

The Square-tailed Kite parent is shown here mantling at the approach of a person to the hide. All the fierce signals are there – the beak, eyes and forbidding posture. Even so, the bird looks a little befuddled by the role it is trying to play. The Square-tailed Kite, like the Crested Hawk, is one of the gentler raptors and seems to find difficulty in assuming a blood-thirsty demeanour.

Raoul

COLLARED SPARROWHAWK, WOODANILLING, WESTERN AUSTRALIA
Hasselblad ELM, 250mm, 1/125th sec, f8, Ektachrome 64, two front flashes

Birds of prey project a sense of mystique. They evoke in people a feeling of power and romance. People often seem to identify with eagles, hawks and falcons - the hooked beak, far-seeing eyes and speed of flight seem to stir some subliminal gene.

At the nest, birds of prey are surprisingly loving towards their chicks. The stereotype of the cruel hawk just does not fit a mother that softly chirps her chicks to sleep. I watched this sparrowhawk use her powerful beak to groom the tiny balls of fluff that were her babies. The challenge, then, in photographing a bird of prey at the nest, is to capture some of its contradictory character, at the same time ferocious and gentle.

Raoul

COLLARED SPARROWHAWK, YABBAGOODI, NEAR DERBY, WESTERN AUSTRALIA
Pentax, 135mm, 1/60th sec, f11, Kodachrome 25, Multiblitz two heads

Peter

If I had to pick a favourite bird it would be hard to differentiate between the Spotted Harrier, the Australian Hobby (which I usually think of as the Little Falcon) and the Collared Sparrowhawk. Of the three I have spent most time with the sparrowhawk and have had many wonderful experiences with many individuals. It is the tamest of the Australian birds of prey, or perhaps I should say the least concerned with human presence. It is possible to photograph a pair at the nest without a hide, but I prefer the traditional way as there is no chance then of aberrant behaviour. This is my favourite sparrowhawk shot, showing the female screaming at some Red-tailed Black-Cockatoos that were flying overhead.

Peter

Raoul

IMMATURE WHISTLING KITE WHISTLING, SHADY CAMP, NORTHERN TERRITORY
Canon F1, 500mm, 1/250th sec, f5.6, Ektachrome Elite 100

One of the best ways to gain access to a bird is to approach from the water, because foreground clutter is eliminated if the bird is on the water's edge. Boats, particularly a small flat-bottomed punt, can be used to glide close and the view can be fantastic. This kite, in its beautiful immature plumage, was photographed on a morning we spent punting around a Top End billabong. The area is frequented by barramundi fishermen and the birds and crocodiles are habituated to people. One Comb-crested Jacana was so tame that I reached out and touched it (unwise, considering the area's legendary jumping crocodiles!). The kite allowed the boat within ten metres and was relaxed enough to concentrate on calling to its parents. I lay on my stomach in the bilge water, rested the lens on the camera bag and photographed as a friend paddled the boat closer.

Raoul

BROWN GOSHAWK, WONGONG GORGE, WESTERN AUSTRALIA

Peter

Praktica, 135mm, 1/60th sec, f8, Kodachrome

This was the first bird of prey I photographed and I didn't really know what to expect. Basically it turned out to be no different from any other bird - I shouldn't have been surprised at the gentleness displayed by the female to her chicks but I was. She couldn't have been more considerate, sheltering them from sun and rain, feeding each in turn, and generally being a loving mother. Most of the prey brought to the nest was little rabbits killed by the male, a more diminutive bird than his mate. Once the chicks were well grown, the female went hunting as well and the pair provided about five rabbits per day, with an occasional bird for variety.

Peter

BROWN GOSHAWK BRUSHING CHICKS WITH EUCALYPT SPRIG, WONGONG GORGE, ARMADALE, WESTERN AUSTRALIA
Praktica, 135mm, 1/60th sec, f8, Kodachrome

Perhaps the most unusual thing I noticed in three weeks of photography at the goshawk nest was the occasion when the female was annoyed by flies attracted by the small rabbit she was dissecting for her hungry eyasses. She flew off and returned with a small twig of eucalyptus leaves, which she brushed over the brood – I can't remember how long the action lasted, but it must have been more than ten seconds as I was able to take a few shots. Later the leaves were worked into the nest.

Peter

LETTER-WINGED KITE, MORNEY CREEK, NEAR WINDORAH, QUEENSLAND *Peter*
Mamiya RB67, 1/250th sec, f11, Ektachrome 100, Metz two heads

LETTER-WINGED KITE, MORNEY CREEK, NEAR WINDORAH, QUEENSLAND *Peter*
Mamiya RB67, 1/250th sec, f11, Ektachrome 100, Metz two heads

This elegant owl-like bird has adopted a way of life in Western Queensland that teeters on the brink of disaster. Its main source of food is one species of rodent, the Long-haired Rat, that inhabits the Channel Country and is subject to periodic irruptions of population, occurring in millions after a good season. The kites congregate in colonies, breeding rapidly while the rats last. To capture their prey, the kites have become nocturnal in habit. They are the only species of birds of prey in the world to hunt at night. The rat populations crash almost overnight and the kites have to spread out in a struggle to survive. Many probably die, but there are always enough "islands" of plenty among the channels where a few rats and kites can hang on until the next good season.

Peter

LETTER-WINGED KITE, MORNEY CREEK, NEAR WINDORAH, QUEENSLAND
Mamiya RB67, 1/250th sec, f11, Ektachrome 100, Metz two heads

Ray Garstone and I visited a colony of kites on Morney Creek, where I took these shots at night, using a red filter over a torch to focus. It seemed to me that a rat was about as big a prey as the kite could handle. When bringing one to its chicks, the bird had to fly in circles, gradually increasing height on straining wings until it could crash-land on the side of the nest. I went back to the colony several times. On my last visit there were no rats and only one kite. The nests were covered with Bearded Dragon skins, so it appeared that the rats had crashed while there were still chicks to be fed, and lizards were the only obvious alternative. It would be interesting to know if they were caught at night or during the day.

Peter

Peter

NANKEEN KESTREL, KELMSCOTT, WESTERN AUSTRALIA
Linhof, 270mm, 1/125th sec, f11, Ektachrome, two front flashes

Kestrels usually nest in hollow trees and are the easiest raptors to find. During the extended courtship period, from June or July until late August, the female does little hunting, but sits on a conspicuous perch waiting for the male to feed her. At Kelmscott, in Western Australia, one pair of kestrels very considerately nested not too high up in a dead tree near our house. I borrowed some old timber from our landlord to build a very rickety structure alongside the tree. I like to build a hide slowly, so the birds get used to it gradually and the process took some time.

NANKEEN KESTREL, KELMSCOTT, WESTERN AUSTRALIA
Linhof, 270mm, 1/125th sec, f11, Ektachrome, two front flashes

Peter

When the tower was only half built, the landlord started demanding his timber back. He didn't want to use it, just wanted it back. I kept putting him off, the structure meanwhile getting higher and higher until after ten days the hide was ready. I was sitting there waiting for the kestrel to return when a truck drove into the paddock. "I've come to get my timber!" the landlord yelled up at me. "Won't be long," I said and he drove off muttering. I got my picture, but it was close. After that we had a portable tower made, which we carry on the car roof-rack.

Peter

PACIFIC BAZA, GULUGUBA, QUEENSLAND
Mamiya RB67, 250mm, 1/250th sec, f5.6, Ektachrome, two flashes

Peter

We lived on "Wallace Brae" at Guluguba for a year and had a wonderful time as the area is rich in birds of prey and friendly people. This baza, or Crested Hawk, nested virtually in our backyard. Jack Cupper, who with his son Lindsay was at that time preparing the classic *Hawks in Focus*, heard about it and drove up non-stop from Mildura with one of his incredible towers. Jack spent some days photographing and also introduced Raoul, who was eight at the time, to bird photography, setting him up in the tower (see page 29). David Hollands, who was also working on a masterly book about birds of prey, came up from Orbost, and I managed the odd shot. The birds reminded me of pigeons rather than raptors, so here we have coupled my picture with Raoul's shot of the Peaceful Dove to show that it is not such a fanciful idea.

Peter

PEACEFUL DOVE AND CHICKS, KANGAROO GULLY, QUEENSLAND (*Raoul*)
Mamiya RB67, 250mm + 50mm extension tube,
1/125th sec, f11, Fujichrome 100, two front flashes

LAUGHING KOOKABURRA, ANSTEAD, QUEENSLAND
Nikon F90, 300mm, auto-focus and auto-exposure at f4, Ektachrome

Peter

Peter

Kookaburras are among the easiest birds to photograph, as they become very tame around human habitation, so easy in fact that there is a temptation to overlook them as subjects for the camera. I can't resist them however and spend too much time chasing them, hoping for the unique shot. I have hundreds of non-unique exposures to choose from so picked these for no better reason than that they were taken under appalling lighting conditions on a wet and windy day, testing to the ultimate the possibilities of the camera. The little picture essay shows a kookaburra not entirely sure whether or not it should share a juicy morsel.

Peter

SACRED KINGFISHER, BELLBOWRIE, QUEENSLAND
Hasselblad ELM, 250mm + 50mm extension tube, 1/125th sec, f11, Fujichrome 100, two front flashes, backlight, photocell

Raou

Peter

BUFF-BREASTED PARADISE-KINGFISHER, INNISFAIL, QUEENSLAND
Linhof, 270mm, 1/250th sec, f11, Ektachrome, two flashes

I had a print of H.C. Richter's lithograph of the Buff-breasted Paradise-Kingfisher from Gould's *Supplement to the Birds of Australia*, and thought it the best painting I'd ever seen, vowing to photograph the bird itself one day. When I read a paper by Mrs Billie Gill about her experiences with the species at Innisfail I persuaded my long-suffering wife that we should move from Western Australia to North Queensland. Billie showed us the kingfisher in a patch of rainforest near her home and pointed out a nest, where we built a hide. My first views confirmed that it is one of Australia's most beautiful birds, but not much like Richter's painting, which shows the long white tail feathers in a graceful curve, and misses out on a few other details. From the hide I could examine the birds at very close range, and noticed that the red area in front of the eye, which looks like bare skin from a distance, actually consists of short bristles. Coming from the aridity of the West, I took some time to get used to the constant rain. I was constantly soaked in the hide, aware that I was sitting on a potentially lethal flash unit that shorted constantly with a sound like a .303 rifle firing. So, although I spent a lot of time photographing, I only got a few pictures because of the electronic problems.

Peter

Raoul

RAINBOW BEE-EATER, IPSWICH, QUEENSLAND
Hasselblad ELM, 250mm + 25mm extension tube, 1/125th sec, f11, two front flashes, one backlight, photocell

Raoul

TURNING ROUND, RAINBOW BEE-EATER, MOGGILL FERRY, QUEENSLAND
Hasselblad ELM, 250mm + 25mm extension tube, 1/125th sec, f8, front flashes

"Turning Round" was taken when I was 14, and was my first attempt at photographing a bird in flight. My father took me through the principles. I set up the camera and flashes with no idea of how effective they would be. The best evidence of my touch is in the position of the bird. With youthful reflexes, I recognised that the bird was contorting itself into an unusual posture and tripped the shutter. The photo opposite, taken seven years later, shows more sophisticated lighting and is sharper, results achieved through constant practice. Again the position is unusual, but this time as a result of the placement of the photocell. Each time the bird left the nest, it turned to look over its far shoulder. Only this once did it turn towards the camera. This picture has special associations for me. The nest was in a sand quarry and my father and I were perched on the edge one afternoon letting the photocell do its thing. In front of us unravelled a magnificent sunset. White-backed Swallows, bee-eaters and kestrels flew like angels in front of God-rays. I look at this photo and remember sharing that sunset with my father.

Raoul

SPOTTED BOWERBIRD, CUNNAMULLA, QUEENSLAND
Hasselblad ELM, 250mm, 1/125th sec, f11, Ektachrome 64, two front flashes and toplight

Raoul

Bowerbirds are such bizarre creatures that I can watch them for hours, transfixed. The male owner of a bower will spend most the day building, painting, and rearranging ornaments in preparation for the female's visit. When she arrives, he will go into paroxysms of dance to impress her. The best ornaments are displayed and he makes himself beautiful for her. The Spotted Bowerbird favours a wide bower of straw decorated with green fruits, sheep bones, broken glass and bullet shells. His best feature, the lilac nape of the neck, is usually hidden from view but is fanned out at the female's approach. The Satin Bowerbird chooses blue objects and likes to paint the inside of the bower with pigments crushed in his beak. I have seen dry Hoop Pine needles used for this purpose. When excited, the male seems to expand, his eyes bulge out and he surrounds the female with a loud sound reminiscent of an electronic eggbeater.

Raoul

SATIN BOWERBIRD, LAMINGTON NATIONAL PARK, QUEENSLAND (*Raoul*)
Hasselblad ELM, 250mm, 1/125th sec, f16, Ektachrome 64, two front flashes,
one toplight, two flashes on background

CUCKOO CHICK PUSHING ROBIN'S EGG OUT OF NEST, CUNNAMULLA, QUEENSLAND
Canon F1, 100mm macro, 1/60th sec, f16, Kodachrome 64, one flash on camera

Raoul

JUVENILE BRUSH CUCKOO, MOGGILL, QUEENSLAND
Pentax, 400mm, 1/125th sec, f5.6, Kodachrome

Peter

Peter

ADULT BRUSH CUCKOO CALLING, MOGGILL, QUEENSLAND
Pentax, 400mm, 1/250th sec, f5.6, Ektachrome

Peter

FEMALE WESTERN SPINEBILL FEEDING PALLID CUCKOO CHICK, KELMSCOTT, WESTERN AUSTRALIA
Practika, 400mm, no exposure data, Kodachrome

Cuckoos make interesting subjects, particularly when being fed by smaller foster-parents. We found a spinebill pair attending a gross Pallid Cuckoo fledgling in our backyard. They brought tiny insects, which they poked right down the cuckoo's throat, almost disappearing in the process. I find it hard to believe that the spinebills actually reared the cuckoo, because they would have difficulty supplying sufficient mass of food. Possibly they took over from larger foster-parents. Cuckoo chicks have a particularly pervasive begging call-note, inspiring birds other than the foster-parents to feed them. The spinebills may have lost their own chicks and begun feeding the cuckoo; being very aggressive, they probably eventually drove the original foster-parents away.

Peter

INLAND THORNBILL, ROCKINGHAM, WESTERN AUSTRALIA   *Peter*
LINHOF, 270mm, 1/250th sec, f16, Ektachrome 64, two front flashes

These two photographs show plainly coloured birds which nevertheless appeal to
me as very attractive. The Inland Thornbill was not very far inland, nesting in the
skirts of a grass-tree about one kilometre from the sea. The chick, whose bill is just
visible in the well-camouflaged nest, was a bronze-cuckoo. The other picture was
taken after I mentioned to Cyril Webster, one of Queensland's better
photographers, my wish to photograph a Little Shrike-thrush. He obligingly found
a nest, at a convenient height from the ground, and set up a hide. I spent a day at
his Goomboorian farm, dodging showers, waiting for the right moment. When I
saw a bird approaching with a choice green caterpillar I hoped that would be it.
Because the thrushes popped the food into their chicks' mouths as soon as they
alighted on the side of the nest, I prefocused on a spot where I hoped they would
land and fired as soon as either bird touched down. Usually they were a centimetre
or so off, but this time the male bird hit the spot and thanks to Cyril and Fay
Webster I got the shot I wanted.

Peter

LITTLE SHRIKE-THRUSH, GOOMBOORIAN, QUEENSLAND (*Peter*)
Mamiya RB67, 250mm + extension tube, 1/250th sec, f8,
Ektachrome, two front flashes, two backlights

WILLY WAGTAIL ON NEST, WOODANILLING, WESTERN AUSTRALIA
Linhof, 270mm, 1/10th sec, f5.6, Ektachrome

Peter

Peter

WILLY WAGTAIL BATHING IN RAIN, ANSTEAD, QUEENSLAND
Pentax, 400mm, 1/60th sec, f5.6, Ektachrome

Black and white birds are difficult to photograph in good light - to get detail in the white results in lack of detail in the black and vice versa. Low light seems to give the best results, but then movement becomes a problem. Both of these pictures were made at very slow shutter speeds in very soft light while it was raining. The movement in the bathing shot adds to the story, emphasising the vigorous flapping that birds indulge in to get thoroughly wet. We have several bird baths in our yards and the Willy Wagtails always came at the same time every day to bathe, even when it was raining heavily and they were already soaking wet. Alas, the Noisy Miners have driven them away and we are entertained by them no more.

Peter

EASTERN YELLOW ROBIN SITTING, MOGGILL STATE FOREST, QUEENSLAND
Hasselblad ELM, 250mm + 25mm extension tube, 1/125th sec, f8, Ektachrome 64, two front flashes, one backlight, one flash on background

Raoul

Peter

WESTERN YELLOW ROBIN, WOODANILLING, WESTERN AUSTRALIA
Practisix, 300mm, 1/25th sec, f16, Ektachrome, two front flashes

When we used to visit Ray and Joan Garstone at Woodanilling many years ago, most of our time was spent at the golf course, not playing golf, of course, but using it as God intended, namely for photographing birds.

Perhaps it is a case of remembering things as better "back in the old days" than they really were, but in my fond memories the Woody Golf Course remains as one of the best places I have encountered for taking pictures of nesting birds, possibly because, being open forest, the backgrounds were always good for photography. The robin above is a case in point – the nest was only about 1.5 metres from the ground and had beautiful even lighting behind it. All that was required was to balance the flashlights with the background exposure for a pleasant shot.

Peter

FEMALE RED-CAPPED ROBIN BUILDING NEST, CUNNAMULLA, QUEENSLAND
Hasselblad ELM, 250mm, 1/125th sec, f8/11, Fujichrome 100, two front flashes, one backlight

Raoul

Peter

EASTERN YELLOW ROBIN, MOGGILL STATE FOREST, QUEENSLAND
Mamiya RB67, 250mm + 50mm extension tube, 1/25th sec, f8, Ektachrome, two front flashes

A lot of my local birdwatching is done in a seven-hectare patch in the Moggill State Forest. It supports a large population of birds, among them 13 pairs of Yellow Robins. Most of the robins nest twice a year, and some bring out three broods, totalling 50 or more chicks altogether. The timing of the first brood is well synchronised – all birds nest either early or late, depending on the season. On average, chicks leave the nest in the first week of September. Subsequent broods are not synchronised and may appear at any time from November to March. Each pair tends to nest in the same vicinity each year, so they are easy to locate. Care is needed in introducing a hide because the male only visits the nest briefly to feed the female, so takes longer to get used to it. We usually leave the hide 20 or more metres from the nest for three or four days to allow the male plenty of time to see it as part of his territory before we move it closer.

Peter

STRIATED PARDALOTE WITH NESTING MATERIAL, CUNNAMULLA, QUEENSLAND
Canon F1, 500mm, 1/125th sec, f4.5, Kodachrome 64

Raoul

Raoul   JACKY WINTER MEDITATING, CUNNAMULLA, QUEENSLAND
Canon F1, 500mm, 1/60th sec, f4.5, Kodachrome 64

Photos of behaviour rely on the bird being relaxed. All you will see otherwise is an uncomfortable, tight-feathered pose. I watch out for places where birds consistently visit to do particular things - sunbathing, feeding, drinking, washing, anting, dust bathing, courting - and try to move in close to their action without disturbing them.

Nests are an obvious focus of activity. I like the Jacky Winter shown here because it is so totally relaxed. All is at peace in this Jacky Winter's world. That in itself is an interesting piece of behaviour. We don't often see animals relaxing without a care, except perhaps for domestic cats.

The red-tipped form of the Striated Pardalote opposite was bringing lining for its nest in an old casuarina tree perched on the edge of a dam. The halo of blue around the pardalote helps the photo, but the real interest lies in the grass in its beak.

Raoul

131

WHITE-THROATED WARBLER, KANGAROO GULLY, QUEENSLAND
Hasselblad ELM, 250mm + 25mm extension tube, 1/250th sec, f8, two front flashes, one backlight

Raoul

Raoul

BLACK-HEADED PARDALOTE, MOGGILL STATE FOREST, QUEENSLAND
Hasselblad ELM, 250mm + 50mm extension tube, 1/500th sec, f11, two front flashes, one backlight

High speed photography reveals amazing things. I am always intrigued by the delicacy and strength revealed by feathers put under the stress of flight. A series of flight photos taken at a nest will reveal the bird in a multitude of positions, as dexterous as a ballet dancer. The best way to take such pictures is with electronic flashes. Even a small Sunpack will go off fast enough. The trouble is that as a flash fires faster it loses brightness, so it must be put closer to the bird. In each of these photos the flashes are barely one metre from the bird. That was only possible because warblers and pardalotes are very tolerant. Even so, a lot of care and patience went into introducing these particular birds to the flashes.

Raoul

SPOTTED PARDALOTE, MOGGILL STATE FOREST, QUEENSLAND
Hasselblad ELM, 250mm + 50mm extension tube, 1/500th sec, f11, two frontlights and one back flash

Nests in tunnels or hollows are the best places to photograph birds in flight. In these situations, the bird has to fly in precisely the same path over and over, allowing camera equipment to be positioned with confidence and then fine-tuned using test pictures taken on polaroid film. Choosing the exact moment to fire is done by eye, either human or electric. I enjoy the challenge to my reflexes that taking flight photos poses. Regrettably, a photoelectric cell set up across the nest entrance produces more consistent results, so this is the method of choice. I console myself by thinking of the bird as taking photos of itself, which is an idea I like.

This pardalote had built in a cliff at the top of a gully. A platform for the camera had to be built by digging into the slope and taking supports out to a tree. The pardalote didn't even seem to notice and went about its business. Petals from a flowering Cassia fell around the nest. Their colours nicely match the yellows of the bird and contribute to the harmony of the picture.

Raoul

Peter

Raoul

RED-BACKED FAIRY-WREN, MOGGILL STATE FOREST, QUEENSLAND

Raoul

Hasselblad ELM, 250mm + 50mm extension tube,1/500th sec, f11, two front flashes, one backlight, one flash on the background

Everywhere the eye looks, it sees details. Even at night the eye can discern shapes in shadow. However, film is relatively insensitive to light and a certain amount must hit it before texture shows. Any less and the film will show black. The eye expects detail in a nature photo and any area of black seems wrong. Black shadows are easily avoided. Having a flash on the opposite side of the camera to the sun, or a flash on each side of the camera will fill in any shadows around the subject. Similarly, a black background may be avoided by adding flash light to it. This photo of the Red-backed Fairy-wren was totally flash lit. There is a flash on either side of the camera, one behind the bird providing backlighting, and another throwing light onto the dead grass in the background. If the picture had been taken with natural light, the whole effect would have lacked colour and depth.

Raoul

Peter

VARIEGATED FAIRY-WREN, MOGGILL STATE FOREST, QUEENSLAND
Mamiya RB67, 250mm + extension tube, 1/250th sec, f8, Ektachrome, Metz 202 two heads

FEMALE SUPERB FAIRY-WREN WITH THRIP, BELLBOWRIE, QUEENSLAND *Raoul*
Hasselblad ELM, 250mm + 50mm extension tube, 1/125th sec, f11, Ektachrome 64, two front flashes, one backlight

The male Splendid Fairy-wren is a truly magnificent creature, ranging from the southwest of Western Australia through the desert to the inland side of the Great Dividing Range. At the eastern edge of its range it is quite blue, as shown in Raoul's picture on the cover and page 71, but becomes increasingly purple towards the west coast, where I took the shot opposite.

At the nest, as many as five males may assist in feeding the chicks, so the species is a dream to photograph. Occasionally we have seen unattached males intruding into occupied territory carrying blue flowers in their bills, hoping to mate with a female. At one nest I even photographed an intruder male feeding a flower petal to the chicks.

Female wrens are sombrely coloured but have a quiet charm of their own. There are often two or three in a breeding group, but probably only one of them lays eggs and it does the majority of the nest-building and incubation. The others play their part when the chicks hatch, keeping up a steady supply of insect food.

Peter

SPLENDID FAIRY-WREN, WONGONG GORGE, WESTERN AUSTRALIA (*Peter*)
Linhof, 270mm + triple extension, 1/250th sec, f16, Ektachrome, Multiblitz three heads

Raoul SCARLET HONEYEATER, MOGGILL STATE FOREST, QUEENSLAND
Hasselblad ELM, 250mm + 50mm extension tube, 1/500th sec, f8/11, Ektachrome 64, two front flashes

I enjoy taking photos and look forward to receiving the processed film afterwards. In my head is a memory of the subject as it appeared. The difference between that and the actual image on film is always a revelation. The two rarely coincide, although with practice I have an improved idea of the finished product. Admittedly, the main thing that I have learned is not to expect too much! The initial edit of the photos is extremely important in the learning process and I think hard all the time I am editing about how the photos could have been improved. This is the time to be harsh. Anything unsharp, uninteresting or poorly-lit hits the bottom of the bin with a satisfying "clang". There are exceptions – images that are imperfect but catch the eye. These I leave and come back to in one month. If they still appeal, they go into a box labelled "near misses". The photos here are two off the top of that pile. The Noisy Miner is sharp, bright and wears the classic grumpy expression of its species. Unfortunately, the background is black, something I dislike in a daylight shot. The Scarlet Honeyeater is slightly blurred. In its favour is a fabulous pose and striking colour

Raoul

NOISY MINER IN UMBRELLA TREE, BRISBANE, QUEENSLAND (*Raoul*)
Mamiya RB67, 250mm + 25mm extension tube, 1/250th sec, f11, Fujichrome 100, two front flashes

RED WATTLEBIRD, KINGS PARK, PERTH, WESTERN AUSTRALIA   *Peter*
Nikon F90, 300mm, auto-focus and auto-exposure at f4, Ektachrome

GREY BUTCHERBIRD   *Peter*
Nikon F90, 300mm, auto-focus and auto-exposure at f4, Ektachrome

When we stumbled across the Golden-backed Honeyeater's nest shown opposite, it was only the second that had been recorded. It came to our notice because we were watching a Rufous-throated Honeyeater building a nest when a Golden-backed flew up and stole some of the material. We followed it and eventually located the drooping spray of bloodwood leaves where it was finishing off a neat nest. While we watched, five birds came with nesting material. We kept an eye on the site and once the chicks had hatched we built a rough tower alongside. John Hutchinson called in to see us and mentioned that he was interested in taking up recording birdcalls, so we took him out to the Golden-backed nest. The birds obliged beautifully, singing their delightful bubbling song while John held his mike ten centimetres away. Since then, John has recorded hundreds, if not thousands, of birds, but I can guarantee none was easier than that first one. The two pictures above were taken opportunistically while walking through the bush looking for whatever turned up. I chose these two examples because the fortuitous wisps of leaves add delicacy to the results. Modern cameras make this sort of picture much easier to take than when I started, but the results aren't much different. Even with modern equipment, a sturdy tripod is still essential.

Peter

Peter

GOLDEN-BACKED HONEYEATER, DERBY, WESTERN AUSTRALIA
Pentax, 135mm, 1/60th sec, f11, Kodachrome, two front flashes

BELL MINERS, MOGGILL STATE FOREST, QUEENSLAND

Raoul

Hasselblad ELM, 250mm + 25mm extension tube, 1/500th sec, f11, Ektachrome 64, two front flashes, one backlight

For many years I maintained a waterhole down in the Moggill State Forest, taking a bucket of water there every day to top it up and keeping a permanent hide there. During the course of a day many hundreds of birds of a score or more species visited to bathe or drink. Probably the prize visitor was the Rose Robin. I took plenty of frames of females and young males, but only once had a magnificent male in my viewfinder. He looked so beautiful I forgot to press the shutter.

Peter

ZEBRA FINCH, NEAR MT. SONDER, NORTHERN TERRITORY
Nikon F90, 300mm, 1/250th sec, f4, Pronia

Perhaps a dozen wool-bale hides and several folding stools were stolen over the years, but they were returned one day, after I met some boys playing there and explained to them what I was doing. On another occasion when I was carting water down I found an uninvited photographer in the hide – he actually told me off for scaring the birds away.

The Zebra Finch above was photographed at a small drying waterhole in the West MacDonnell Ranges. Because the weather was moderately hot we had to be extremely careful that our hide didn't keep away the more timid individuals among the thousands of birds visiting the water. So we limited our photographic sessions to two hours then moved the hide away. Nevertheless, the time spent there was the most productive that I recall.

Peter

LEWIN'S HONEYEATER, MOGGILL STATE FOREST, QUEENSLAND
Hasselblad ELM, 250mm + extension tube, 1/500th sec, f8, Ektachrome 64, two front flashes

Raoul

Raoul FUSCOUS HONEYEATER AND CHICK, MOGGILL STATE FOREST, QUEENSLAND
Hasselblad ELM, 250mm + extension tube, 1/500th, f8/11 sec, Ektachrome 64, two front flashes, one backlight flash

These photos were taken at a small waterhole in eucalypt forest when I was about 15. I had been photographing birds seriously for two years. Up to that time, my main enjoyment had come from sharing the outdoors with my father. The birds themselves were of less interest, although I remember wishing for a girlfriend as elegant and cheerful as a female Variegated Fairy-wren. Then I spent a series of afternoons after school enthralled by the stream of birds that came into this waterhole. From two metres away, I watched dozens of Scarlet, White-naped, White-throated, Black-chinned and Lewin's Honeyeaters, Brown Pigeons, Bellbirds, Golden Whistlers, Yellow Robins and, most endearingly, White-throated Tree-creepers, whose long toes forced them to shuffle backwards into the water.

On one particular afternoon, a clutch of Fuscous Honeyeater chicks just out of the nest followed their parents down to the water for their first bath. They went berserk and joyfully played in the water. Their exuberance was infectious. By the time the tiny, sodden balls of fluff had flown off, I knew that my future would involve photographing birds.

Raoul

FEMALE BLACK HONEYEATER, CUNNAMULLA, QUEENSLAND

Raoul

Mamiya RB67, 360mm, 1/60th sec, f8, two front light flashes minus 1 stop, sun from behind

Light can come from many directions. Birds, like people, tend to look best in diffused light, like that found on an overcast day, or with backlighting that produces a romantic halo. Both types of lighting are illustrated here with photos of the same species. Both images are lit with flash and sun, although in one the sun shines from behind onto the bird and nest, while in the other the sun lights only the background. The trick is to push enough flash light into the dark areas without overpowering the sunlight (see "synchro sun", page 21). The backlighting above enhances the textures of a beautiful nest site, which makes you wonder if birds have their own sense of aesthetics. The other photo's softness compliments a demure bird, who leaves the flashy, jet-fighter displays to her crisply patterned mate.

Raoul

Raoul

FEMALE BLACK HONEYEATER, BOLLON, QUEENSLAND
Hasselblad ELM, 250mm, 1/125th sec, f8/11, two front light flashes

CRIMSON CHAT, CUNNAMULLA, QUEENSLAND
Hasselblad ELM, 250mm, 1/125th sec, f11, Ektachrome 64, two front flashes, one backlight

Raoul

Photography is both a physical and a mental game. Practice makes its execution flow at a level almost below conscious thought. The hand reaches automatically for the correct knob and turns it just the right degree without thinking. I love the feeling that comes from looking at a situation and knowing within a second exactly how all the technical and natural elements will come together into an effortless-looking photo.

The picture of the chat above was taken at the end of a trip to the mulga country. After two weeks of constant photography, the process of setting up the hide at this nest was smooth and efficient. The birds were hardly disturbed and proved to be relaxed and beautiful subjects. The most satisfying aspect of the resulting picture for me is the lighting, which has a subtlety achieved only with practice.

Raoul

Peter

CRIMSON CHAT, MURCHISON RIVER, WESTERN AUSTRALIA
Linhof, 270mm, 1/500th sec, f16, Ektachrome 64, two front flashes, photocell release

151

SILVEREYES AT ROOST, INNISFAIL, QUEENSLAND

Peter

Praktisix, 180mm, exposure details not recorded

Peter

HOUSE SPARROW, ANSTEAD, QUEENSLAND
Pentax, 400mm, 1/25th sec, f5.6, Ektachrome

While it is nice to get away into the wilderness, there are plenty of opportunities around the home for taking pictures. The silvereyes opposite were found roosting at night only one metre from the ground. When I took the first shot, the flash must have woken them, so I took another as they blearily looked around before they decided it was just lightning and went back to sleep.

The House Sparrow is an introduced species and something of a pest but is nevertheless a bird and not to be entirely overlooked. I set myself the unrewarding task of taking an interesting picture of one and after many tries came up with this, taken through a spray of wattle blossoms.

Peter

FEMALE CRIMSON FINCH, FOGG DAM, NORTHERN TERRITORY
Canon F1, 500mm + 50mm extension tube, 1/60th sec, f4.5, Ektachrome Elite 100

Raoul

Raoul

MALE CRIMSON FINCH, FOGG DAM, NORTHERN TERRITORY
Canon F1, 500mm + 50mm extension tube, 1/60th sec, f4.5, Kodachrome 200, taken from car window

The first Crimson Finches that flashed across my path stunned me with their bright colour. I had just arrived in the Northern Territory and had immediately headed to Fogg Dam, a birdwatching haven. The finches proved to be plentiful and confiding, so I set myself the goal of a full-frame, sharp photo of a male. As they are tiny birds, an extension tube was needed to allow close enough focus, for even with a telephoto lens I had to be about four metres away to fill the frame. Although tame, the Crimson Finch doesn't stay still for long, so the task proved to be difficult. I have made about 25 trips to Fogg Dam in the last two years in pursuit of the goal, managing many rolls of near misses – too small, too dark, out of focus or leaves in the way. These two efforts are my best so far, but I'm hoping that by going back better ones will be forthcoming.

Wherever I have lived, there has been a patch of bush close to town that has been worth repeated visits. If I return time and again, opportunities may be discovered and fully explored. I know that, if I persevere, one day the unusual will happen when the camera is ready.

Raoul

155

FEMALE FIGBIRD EATING CARPENTARIA PALM BERRY, TOP END, NORTHERN TERRITORY
Canon AE1, 500mm + 50mm extension tube, 1/250th sec, f4.5, Kodachrome 200

Raoul

The female Figbird shown above is really struggling to swallow that berry, her beak pushed beyond its normal limit. Look at the way her face has begun to distort: there seems to be a risk that her eye will pop out! A photo like this makes me marvel at how graceful and how grotesque birds can be, alien creatures full of surprise and magic. Every feather is a delight. Photographing birds allows me to share with others the sense of wonder birds have aroused in my soul. I hope that this book has similarly inspired you to watch and record the birds in your life.

Raoul

Raoul

MALE FIGBIRD, TOP END, NORTHERN TERRITORY
Canon F1, 500mm, 1/250th sec, f4.5, Ektachrome Elite 100

ACKNOWLEDGEMENTS

Many people have helped me in the production of these photos. My thanks to Luke, Michael, Graham, Rama K, the Harpers, F Stop Colour Lab Brisbane, Technicolour S.A. and the hospital staffs of Royal Hobart, Broken Hill and the RAAF Base, Darwin. I owe a debt to Michael Morcombe, Ray Garstone and Nev Male for their time and example. My love to Michelle for her support and care. Special thanks to Steve and Jan Parish and the team at Steve Parish Publishing for this opportunity. And finally, all my regard and gratitude to my parents, Pat and Peter, for their wisdom, patience and good genes.

Raoul

Most of my friends are photographers or painters of birds and they have contributed enormously to my enjoyment of life. Many of them helped bring the images in this book to fruition, especially Steve and Jan Parish, Ray and Joan Garstone, Michael and Irene Morcombe, Graeme and Pam Chapman, Colin and Ali Lloyd, Eric and Del Lindgren, Eric and Margaret McCrum, Billie Gill, Kevn and Peg Griffiths, Wilf and Lucy Clinch, Ken and Joan Else, Cyril and Fay Webster, Evan and Kay Williams, Jack Cupper, the Squelch family and the Woodside family. Roy Caruth, Wilf Clinch and Doug Dow made and repaired various photographic gadgets, earning my eternal gratitude. My uncle, Ted Yates, gave me a photo-cell which still works perfectly after 30 years. Thanks also to Greg Sullivan for his masterly conversion of our photographs to colour separations, and to Holly Bambridge for her sympathetic design. Special thanks to the production crew. Above all, my thanks to my parents, Sam and Nell, and particularly to my wife Pat, who assisted with the majority of these pictures. And, dear reader, instead of interesting times, may I wish you a son like Raoul.

Peter

PHOTOGRAPHING AUSTRALIA'S BIRDS

• Raoul Slater • Peter Slater •

Raoul

Peter

Peter Slater took up photographing birds at an early age, eventually capturing more than 400 species on film. He won more than 50 medals in International Salons of Photography and was made an *Artiste de la Fédération Internationale de l'Art Photographique* in 1964. Since the publication of his *Field Guide to Australian Birds*, he has concentrated on painting birds fulltime.

Raoul Slater also had an early introduction to photography and quickly made his mark in National and International Salons, winning numerous awards. While still at school he became both a Licentiate and an Associate of the Australian Photographic Society. Now a physiotherapist, Raoul spends his spare time photographing birds, and recording landscapes with large format cameras.

Whenever possible, father and son meet in some remote area of Australia and together pursue their mutual passion – producing the best possible images of wild birds in their natural habitat.

OTHER TITLES IN THE STEVE PARISH PUBLISHING PHOTOGRAPHING AUSTRALIA BOOK SERIES

PRODUCTION DETAILS

Photography and text - Peter Slater, Raoul Slater
Editing - Pat Slater, Steve Parish Publishing
Artwork - Holly Bambridge, Steve Parish Publishing

Printed in Australia - Fergies
Binding - Podlich Enterprises

First published in Australia by Steve Parish Publishing Pty Ltd
PO Box 2160 Fortitude Valley BC Queensland 4006
© Copyright Steve Parish Publishing Pty Ltd
© Copyright photography and text
Peter and Raoul Slater, 1995

National Library of Australia cataloguing in publication data:
Slater, Peter and Slater, Raoul - Photographing Australia's Birds
ISBN 875932 07 0
1. Photography - Australia
2. Title - Photographing Australia's Birds